The Nap

by Isabella Jenkins
illustrated by Erik Hobson

Practice Pre-Decodable 5

McGraw Hill Education

Bothell, WA • Chicago, IL • Columbus, OH • New York, NY

MHEonline.com

Send all inquiries to:
McGraw-Hill Education
8787 Orion Place
Columbus, OH 43240

ISBN: 978-0-02-132207-7
MHID: 0-02-132207-4

Printed in China.

9 10 11 12 13 DSS 27 26 25 24 23

a  and 

rake leaves

a  and a 

cart list

the  and 

hose water

a  and the 

ball net

the 

milk

and the 
cups

the  and a 

chair

nap